CRAZY ABOUT HOCKEY!

Written by Loris Lesynski

Illustrated by Gerry Rasmussen

annick press

Toronto • New York • Vancouver

For teacher/librarian and sportsman Caley Feldman, with thanks for putting together all those "focus groups" of terrifically athletic kids at Chester Public School to help me with my hockey (*and* soccer *and* basketball) poems. —LL

© 2015 Loris Lesynski (text)
© 2015 Gerry Rasmussen (illustrations)
Design & Art Direction by Loris Lesynski, Laugh Lines Design

Annick Press Ltd.

We acknowledge the support of the Canada Council for the Arts, the Ontario Arts Council, and the Government of Canada through the Canada Book Fund (CBF) for our publishing activities.

ONTARIO ARTS COUNCIL
CONSEIL DES ARTS DE L'ONTARIO
an Ontario government agency
un organisme du gouvernement de l'Ontario

Cataloging in Publication
Lesynski, Loris, author
    Crazy about hockey! / Loris Lesynski ; illustrated by Gerry Rasmussen.
Poems.
Issued in print and electronic formats.
ISBN 978-1-55451-712-1 (bound).--ISBN 978-1-55451-711-4 (pbk.).--
ISBN 978-1-55451-713-8 (html).--ISBN 978-1-55451-714-5 (pdf)

1. Hockey--Juvenile poetry. I. Rasmussen, Gerry, 1956-, illustrator
II. Title.

PS8573.E79C724 2015   jC811'.54   C2014-905945-0

Distributed in Canada by:
Firefly Books Ltd.
50 Staples Avenue, Unit 1
Richmond Hill, ON
L4B 0A7

Published in the U.S.A. by:
Annick Press (U.S.) Ltd.
Distributed in the U.S.A. by:
Firefly Books (U.S.) Inc.
P.O. Box 1338, Ellicott Station
Buffalo, NY 14205

The artwork in this book was done in pen and ink and Photoshop. The poems are set in Chaparall Pro. Titles are in Bryan Talbot Lower, with page numbers in Shake Open, both from www.comicfonts.com.

Printed in China

Visit us at: www.annickpress.com
Visit the author at: www.lorislesynski.com
Visit the illustrator at: www.gerryrasmussen.com

You can write to Loris c/o Annick Press, 15 Patricia Avenue, Toronto ON M2M 1H9 Canada or e-mail her at LorisLesynski@gmail.com

Also available in e-book format.
Please visit www.annickpress.com/ebooks.html for more details.
Or scan

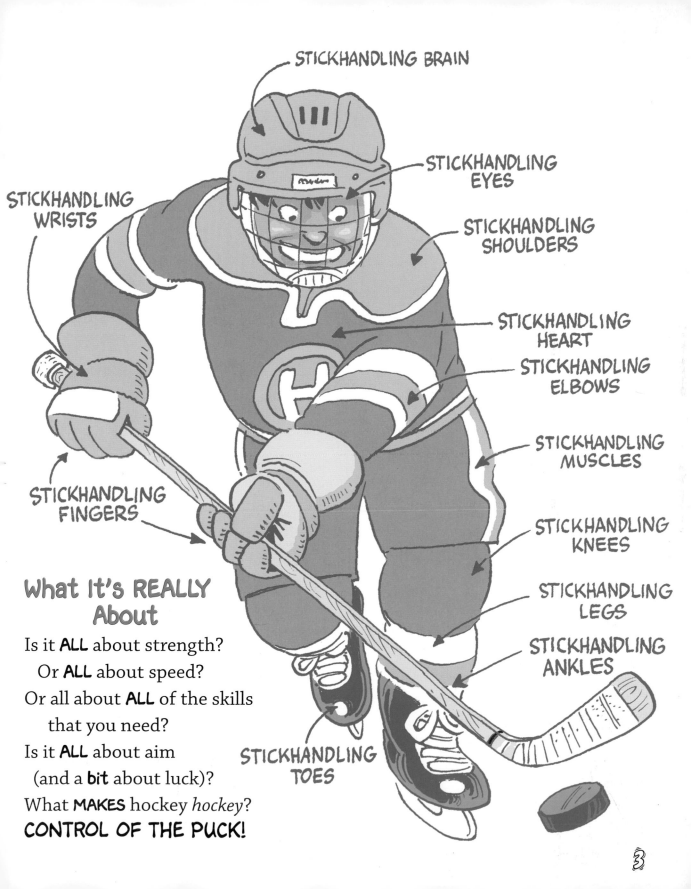

STICKHANDLING BRAIN

STICKHANDLING EYES

STICKHANDLING SHOULDERS

STICKHANDLING WRISTS

STICKHANDLING HEART

STICKHANDLING ELBOWS

STICKHANDLING MUSCLES

STICKHANDLING FINGERS

STICKHANDLING KNEES

STICKHANDLING LEGS

STICKHANDLING ANKLES

STICKHANDLING TOES

What It's REALLY About

Is it **ALL** about strength?
   Or **ALL** about speed?
Or all about **ALL** of the skills
   that you need?
Is it **ALL** about aim
   (and a **bit** about luck)?
What **MAKES** hockey *hockey*?
CONTROL OF THE PUCK!

3

No Game Without It

open a basketball,
what'll be there?
layers of wrapping
and then only air

but pucks have no pieces,
a puck has no parts
in motion the moment
a period starts

a puck is all puck
from the bottom to top
so solid that only the net
makes it stop

a puck is all puck
from the outside to in
a blob with one job: to
get out there and win!

Why WE Win

we gotta get it
all in sync
the way we move
the way we think
a team's all speed
and skills and more
connected: that's
the way to score!
our team becomes
one brilliant brain
so *yes!* we win
another game!

My Team!

We get in position,
   about to start,
around us the thumps
   of every heart—
the hearts on the ice
   and the ones that came
to watch an amazing
   hockey game.
In no other sport
   is the playing as fast—
the furious speed of the puck as
   it's passed!

The atmosphere: electrifying!
Players skate like eagles
   flying!
Precision, decisions,
   momentum and style,
sometimes collisions,
   with five in a pile!
The gloves come off and
   a brawl breaks out.
There's no such thing
   as a game without
emotions ablaze with
   delight and despair,

but *whoa* to those moments
   when tempers flare!
The game goes on,
   even more intense,
for us and the fans,
   an insane suspense.
The puck makes its way to
   a wide open net
then goes off the post
   but it's not over yet
'cause one of us pokes it right
   over the line!

The other team knows that
   they've run out of time.
Our goalie's grinning
   'cause winning's so sweet.
The shouts from the crowd
   can be heard in the street!
Each of us leaves the ice
   and then—
becomes just
   a regular person
      again.

Hoc**K**ey?

Seems it's *packed*

with **K**s

and uses them in countless ways.

LIK**E WHAT?** You know

that **K**ids'll as**K**.

Like s**K**ates, and stic**K**s,

and s**K**ills and mas**K**!

Like strea**K**ing, and de**K**ing,

and then attac**K**

knowing your teammates

have your bac**K**!

Fa**K**ing and hat tric**K**s.

A rin**K**! A wrec**K**!

Of course Canuc**K**s!

A hoo**K**! A chec**K**!

Shot bloc**K**ing, roo**K**ies, and brea**K**away plays—

hoc**K**ey's got a **CRUSH** on **K**s!

The **K** sound in hoc**K**ey—hear how it roc**K**s.

(See one that's ***SNEA**K**Y?***

The **PENALTY BO**K**s!)**

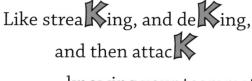

Hockey: A Very Short History

It was thousands and thousands
of years ago
when cavemen hunted on
ice and snow.

The very first skate
that they ever made
used an animal bone
that was carved like a blade.

They must have used strapping
for speed and control,
pushing ahead on the ice
with a pole.

Over the centuries,
skates were improved,
and feet were then able
to turn when they moved.

Did *hockey* begin then?
No, everyone knows
a sport wasn't fun if it
meant that you froze!

What *made* hockey happen,
and then made it better?
When someone invented
the hockey sweater!

The Stanley Cup

1888

A teenager, Isobel Stanley, went
   to Montreal for a winter event.
Saw her first hockey game—love
   at first sight!
Persuaded her brothers
   to play every night,
then went to Lord Stanley,
   said, "Dad, listen up,
how 'bout donating a trophy or cup?
We're crazy for hockey!
   We'd like others, too,
to enjoy it as much as the Stanleys all do!"

Lord Stanley said, "YES, a cup
   could be fun!"
So the very next season,
   the team that won
cheered when its *name* was
   engraved on the cup—
then got the champagne
   and filled it up!

1889

NOW!

A hundred years later,
   the Cup is still here,
bigger and brighter
   with every year.
And the winning team
   with the highest score
can take it home for a week
   or more!

Women in Action

Girls good at hockey?
Totally true.
There's nothing a girl who loves hockey
can't do!
At first, mostly boys were the ones
who would play.
But girls loved the game
in the very same way.
When too many pucks would get
stuck in a fold
of the skirts women wore in
the days of old,
their uniforms changed
to become the same
as the boys', and the girls were
at last in the game.

Places to Play

In olden days the game was played
on ponds and frozen lakes,
with woods around the loudest sound
the grinding of the skates.

Backyards, too, still sometimes do
for homemade rinks outdoors.
Even simple shinny pleases
everyone who scores.

Ball hockey games are not the same,
but mostly on the street
(when *"Car!"* along with *"Score!"* is what
the players most repeat).

12

Modern-day arenas, now—
    they're big, and bright, and loud,
a mountainside of seating for a huge
    and happy crowd.

The ice is slick, and echoes all the cheers
    and boos and grunts.
A thousand fans—and players—
    all excited, *all* at once.

    A pond is cheap and simple,
        fine for practice shooting pucks.
    A really good arena comes to half
        a billion bucks.
            But anywhere it's on, the game's
                as thrilling as can be.
                    (Dad still hits the ceiling when
                        he watches on TV!)

13

Hockey topics? Hundreds!
   Stats? A zillion more!
Stanley Cups, and ups and downs,
   awards and facts galore!
All the books on hockey with
   the records of the day,
and *more* with all the special tips
   of brilliant ways to play.

How did Gretzky know *exactly*
   where the puck would go?
Was Hull's the fastest slap shot in
   those games so long ago?
Which goalie chose to knit himself
   his custom underwear?
A zillion facts on hockey always
   waiting for you there!

If Aliens Came to the Game

SUPPOSE you came from outer space,
  our rink by chance your landing place.
Shiny whiteness ... circles ... lines—
  what messages in those designs?

The life-forms in those wriggling hordes!
  The *whoosh* of skates, the *thumps* on boards!
All the creatures looked the same.
  Your language had no word for "game."

You'd watch us swoop as if with wings.
  You'd see the sticks as living things.
No other world that you'd explored
  had frequent shouting out, **"HE SCORED!"**

Returning to your launching pad,
  you'd scratch your heads (if heads you had)
and say, "That planet's *so* extreme—
  the strangest hunt we've ever seen!
  The creatures there are out of luck.
  They'll **NEVER** catch and eat that puck."

WHAT THE PUCK IS CALLED AROUND THE WORLD:

PUCK!	PUCK!	POC!	PUCK!	PAK!	KIEKKO!	DISCO!
SPANISH	DUTCH	IRISH	TURKISH	CROATIAN	FINNISH	ITALIAN

15

The Uniform-Putting-On Machine

Hockey?

   More equipment

      than in any other sport.

         Skates and socks and pads and cups

            and underwear and shorts!

So putting on a uniform,

   there's lots and lots to do—

pulling, tying, tucking, sticking,

   tightly lacing, too.

     But what if they invented

a machine that got you dressed

   in only seven seconds—

     wouldn't coaches

        be impressed?

16

They once invented velcro.
  Now it's time for something new.
A special spray-on microfiber
  uniform with glue?
Or bubble wrap without a gap,
  a custom-molded kit?
Padding like a hot dog bun
  and guaranteed to fit?

We'll try out almost anything,
  we'll put it on—and **THEN**
once the game is over,
  hope it all comes **OFF** again!

Invisible Drills

Looks just like
I'm sitting still.
No one knows
I'm doing a drill.
But everywhere
throughout the day,
I train
my brain
to stay in play,
to use that mental
discipline
so good for
every game
I'm in.
In history, science,
math, and more
I'm planning how
to shoot and score.
The season's on!
So all the time
it's hockey!
   hockey!
      hockey!
      hockey!
   HOCKEY!!!
         on my mind.

Hockey Uniforms: One Use Only

hockey players
have no pockets
have no place
to put a puck
say you want to
carry something
like a sandwich?
out of luck
gloves can't handle
holding things
you'd always drop
a drink
the *only* place
this uniform
is useful is
the rink!

You Asked about the Mask?

The birth of the mask
came oh so slowly.
Elizabeth Graham,
a brilliant goalie,
eighty-five years ago
wore one to play
though the coach
of her team said,
"You *put* that away!"

She respected the rules, but
loved her teeth more.
She said, "I ***NEED***
this mask before
I ever go *anywhere* near
the net."
Wasn't it time for
protection yet?

Apparently not—
more smacks and hits
(and so many noses
bashed to bits)
till goalie Jacques Plante
(who'd been hurt a lot),
declared, **"I'm not taking
ONE MORE shot!!!"**
The coach was so mad, he said,
"Don't you dare!"
But Plante said, "It's what
we ***all*** should wear."

Then **everyone** said
    it made sense to ask
for the safety supplied
    by a comfortable mask.

    'Cause life goes on *after*
        the game is done,
    and whether you lost
        or whether you won,
    you'd probably want
        to **finish** the game
    with your face still pretty
        much the same.

21

The Puzzle of the Game

WE do all the skating up and down the ice
and back.
WE wear out our eyeballs with the puck
and keeping track.
WE use all our muscles from the hours that we trained.
So how come **DAD'S** exhausted
at the end of every game?

Hockey's Full of Opposites

hot cheeks
cold ice
opponents mean
opponents nice
black skates
white rink
only: move
only: think
forward pass
backhand shot
puck is here
AND THEN
IT'S NOT!!!
OH so *serious*
SO much fun
whether we lost
or (better!!!)
we won

SNAP!

Hockey makes you
make decisions
faster than
the speed of light.
All the time, you're
calculating,
got to get
the angles right.
Change the game in
nanoseconds!
New directions
in a blink!
Everything's so *fast*—
how come we never
melt the rink?

Hockey Emotions

Triumph!
Then sadness.
JOY!
Then despair!
Hockey is
making me
tear out my hair!
Can't you just *watch*
without FEELING
so much?

Nope!

The Xtreme Stick

Once a stick was simple:
just a **stick.**

Anyone could find one,
take your pick.

But over time,
it turned out
wood just wasn't
good enough.

Nowadays, a stick's
a mix of
complicated stuff:
fiberglass, aluminum,
and different kinds
of glue,
graphite, and titanium,
and carbon fiber, too.

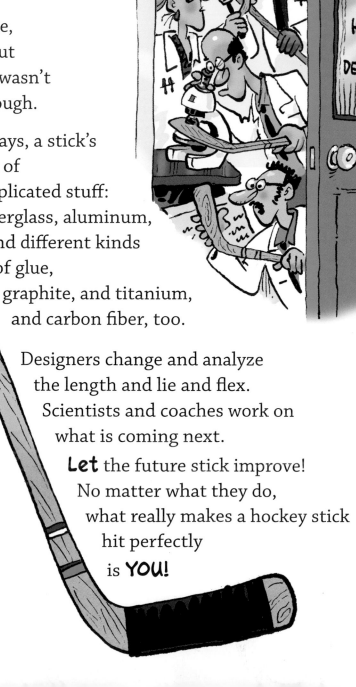

Designers change and analyze
the length and lie and flex.
Scientists and coaches work on
what is coming next.
Let the future stick improve!
No matter what they do,
what really makes a hockey stick
hit perfectly
is **YOU!**

Elbow Fouls

Every player
has to know
exactly
where the elbows go
not stuck out wide
like wings in flight
or tucked in tense
and much too tight,
remembering
an elbow's place
is **never** in
some short kid's
face!

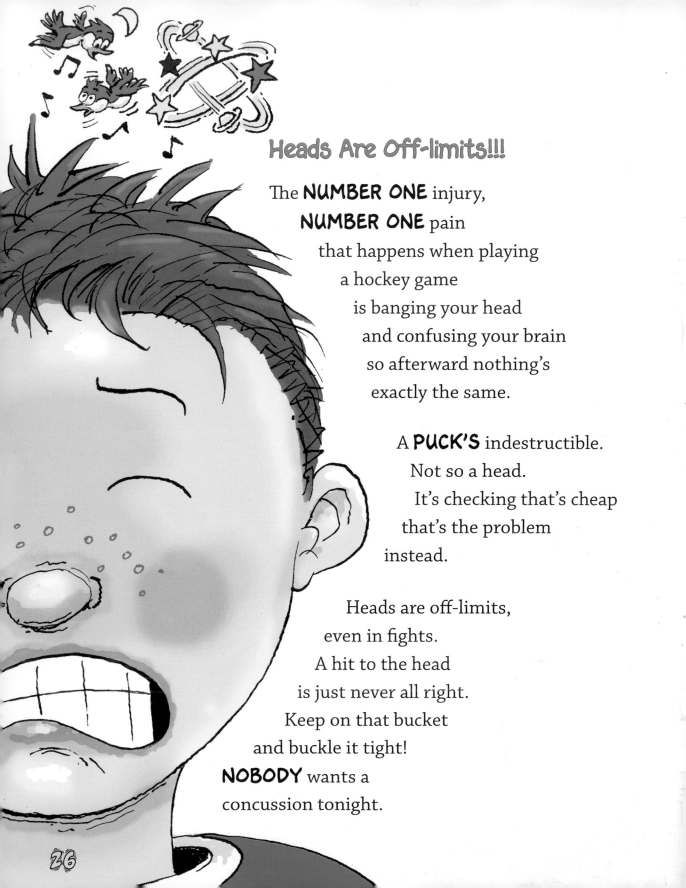

Heads Are Off-limits!!!

The **NUMBER ONE** injury,
NUMBER ONE pain
that happens when playing
a hockey game
is banging your head
and confusing your brain
so afterward nothing's
exactly the same.

A **PUCK'S** indestructible.
Not so a head.
It's checking that's cheap
that's the problem
instead.

Heads are off-limits,
even in fights.
A hit to the head
is just never all right.
Keep on that bucket
and buckle it tight!
NOBODY wants a
concussion tonight.

Miracle Goal

Never before
was a shot
so precise—
the puck flew
like lightning,
high over the ice!
The goalie's eyes crossed,
and he lost a skate.
We couldn't untangle
our ankles till late.
The net seemed to shake
for an hour or more—
not even earthquakes
get *that* kind of score!
That slapshot I made
was as sharp as a knife.
I bet I'll relive it
the rest of my life!

TELL ME ABOUT THAT GOAL AGAIN, GRAMPA!

PLEASE?

PLEASE?

PLEASE?

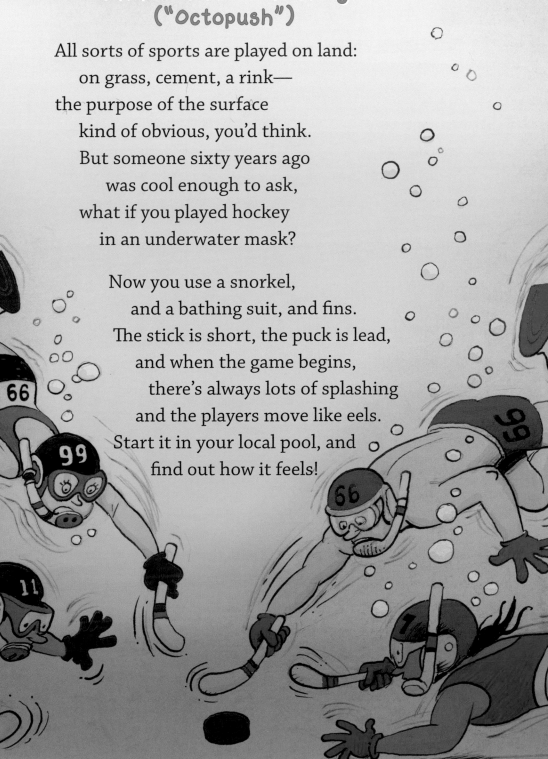

Underwater Hockey
("Octopush")

All sorts of sports are played on land:
    on grass, cement, a rink—
the purpose of the surface
    kind of obvious, you'd think.
But someone sixty years ago
    was cool enough to ask,
what if you played hockey
    in an underwater mask?

Now you use a snorkel,
    and a bathing suit, and fins.
The stick is short, the puck is lead,
    and when the game begins,
    there's always lots of splashing
    and the players move like eels.
Start it in your local pool, and
    find out how it feels!

My Goal:
More Kids on More Ice

I feel so sorry
I feel so sad
for any kids
who never had
the chance to play
this brilliant game
OF HOCKEY!

it's got so much
expensive stuff
that even kids
both fast and tough
might simply not have quite enough
FOR HOCKEY.

27th ANNUAL EQUIPMENT EXCHANGE!

PERFECT!

can uniforms and skates
be shared?
if I become a
millionaire
I'll stock arenas everywhere
MORE HOCKEY!

MAX'S ARENAS

MAX'S ARENAS

MAX'S ARENAS

Invented for Hockey?

It was Mr. Frank Zamboni
who invented the machine
that keeps a rink so smooth and slick,
the ice so nice and clean.

What else could be invented
to improve this awesome game?
If **you're** the one who does it,
you can name it with your name.

Any puck is just like any **other** puck,
it's true,
but **try!** invent a better puck—
they'll name it after you!

Game Over

The ice was so glossy,
    the lights were so bright,
we came out forgetting
    it's already night.
Mom gives a honk from
    the car where it's parked,
snow in the headlights aswirl
    in the dark.
We're leaving the rink
    with a grin, if we won
(and a shrug if we lost
    because still—it was fun),
knowing that practice
    tomorrow, at six,
means we'll be here with
    our bags and our sticks,
ready to play, though
    the morning's like night,
the hockey arena
    our favorite light.

You don't have to be a sports fan to become a fan of these upbeat, bouncy poems by Loris Lesynski!

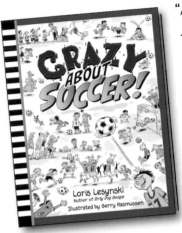

"An ebullient collection of tongue-twisting, imagination-stretching, smile-cracking poems."

–School Library Journal

"Even if you don't play basketball, the rhythms and chants, emotions, and colorful illustrations will win you over to the game."

–CM Reviews

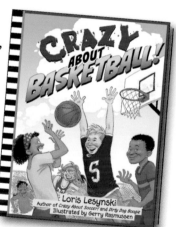

For details on these and other titles by Loris Lesynski,

visit www.annickpress.com

Want MORE hockey poems? Write some of your own!
Find out how at www.crazyabouthockey.ca